I0846062

Custom Clothing Success

Starting and Running a Tailoring Business

Table of Contents

Chapter 1. Introduction

In a world brimming with fashion trends, there's nothing quite like the timeless appeal of a custom-tailored outfit. Welcome to our Special Report on "Custom Clothing Success: Starting and Running a Tailoring Business." Embark on a journey through the endless possibilities that lie within the domain of personal style expression. This eye-opening guide is filled to the brim with fascinating insights, hands-on guidance, and inspirational stories about turning the art of bespoke tailoring into a successful business venture. With an ideal blend of technical detail for industry insiders and a cheerfully engaging narrative for the uninitiated, this report embodies the spirit of entrepreneurial craftsmanship. Boost your knowledge, spur your creativity, and get ready to stitch your way to success with this valuable resource. Get ready, your sartorial adventure begins here!

Chapter 2. Stitching Your Path: An Overview of the Tailoring Business

The world of tailoring is as intricate as the fabric threads woven together to compose a stunning, custom-made attire. It's a delicate balance of various components – technology's role, appropriate equipment, exceptional customer service, and the art and science of the craft itself. In this detailed breakdown, we take you down this path, providing a comprehensive framework for starting and successfully running your tailoring business.

2.1. The Art and Science of Tailoring

Tailoring is not just about cutting and stitching fabric. It's a dedicated process that takes into account the customer's body type, style preferences, and even their personality. Furthermore, it maintains a sharp focus on precision and attention to detail to create a beautiful, personalized garment that fits like a glove.

Understanding the human body, its proportions, and how bodies move are at the core of becoming a successful tailor. You have to be able to conceptualize designs that complement different body types, and then translate these concepts into patterns and finished pieces. Continual learning is vital to staying relevant in the industry. Keep honing your craft, learning about the latest techniques, and studying new materials as they hit the market.

2.2. The Role of Technology

In the age of Digital Darwinism, every business, including tailoring, must adapt and align themselves with emerging technologies.

Computer-Aided Design (CAD) applications are revolutionizing tailoring by providing highly precise and proportionate designs. 3D body scanning solutions deliver meticulous measurements in seconds, reducing human error and improving client satisfaction. Online platforms provide easy customer interfacing and e-commerce solutions. Ensure that you stay up-to-date with these technologies to stay competitive in your business.

2.3. Essential Equipment

For a tailor, having a well-equipped workspace is paramount. Good quality scissors, measuring tape, sewing machine (both domestic and industrial), iron, dress forms, and cutting tables are some basics you can't do without. The importance of investing in quality equipment cannot be overstated. Faulty or imprecise tools can compromise the quality of your work and the customer's satisfaction.

2.4. Understanding Your Customers

Every successful business hinges on understanding its clientele. As a tailor, customers trust you with their sense of style and personal image. Therefore, good communication skills are critical. Develop your ability to listen, understand, advise, and translate a client's desires into the clothing that they want. Clientele handling isn't just a one-time process; it's about building durable, long-term relationships.

2.5. Marketing and Branding Strategies

The tailoring business, more than others, depends on creating and maintaining a solid reputation. Word-of-mouth recommendations are effective, but they must be supplemented with other strategies.

Online presence, social media marketing, participation in local events, and collaborating with related businesses (e.g., wedding planners or luxury brands) are some tactics you can leverage. Proper branding can effectively communicate your values, expertise, and capabilities to potential customers, setting you apart in a competitive market.

2.6. Financial Management

Establishing a system for pricing, bookkeeping, cash flow management, taxation, and financial planning forms the bulwark of your tailoring business. A well-thought-out plan should balance your operating costs with competitive pricing. Using software solutions can assist in keeping track of income, expenses, and profitability.

2.7. Legal Requirements and Compliance

Starting a business involves navigating through local regulations, permits, and licenses. It's crucial to consult with legal counsel to avoid violations and penalties. Additionally, tailoring businesses should also look into getting insurance to mitigate loss from things like theft, damage, or legal claims.

2.8. Sustainability and Ethics

Finally, aligning with sustainable and ethical practices is increasingly important. Using sustainable materials, minimizing waste, advocating fair trade practices can not only build trust and loyalty among customers but also contribute to a better world. Leading with conscience is an ingredient for long-term success in contemporary business.

Starting and running a tailoring business involves juggling multiple components that, when sewn together expertly, carve your path towards success. Becoming a successful tailor isn't just about perfecting the art and science of the craft but also about developing a robust business acumen. It requires the passion of an artist and the mind of a businessperson. With these building blocks, you can tailor your journey to success in the world of custom clothing.

Chapter 3. From Hobby to Business: Nurturing Your Tailoring Passion

Your personal passion for tailoring can be the seed from which a successful business grows. Transforming this hobby into a full-fledged enterprise requires a strong blend of creativity, technical skill, business knowledge, and most importantly, an unyielding commitment to your craft.

3.1. Understanding Your Passion

Firstly, it's important to understand what drives your love for tailoring. Is it the act of creating something beautiful out of a simple piece of fabric? Or the feeling of satisfaction that you get when a client wears something you've created with your own hands? Understanding what fuels your passion is crucial, as it helps keep you motivated and inspires you to push your creative limits.

3.2. Mastering the Craft

While a love for tailoring is a good starting point, you need to combine it with a deep understanding of the craft to succeed in the business. Strive to master different sewing techniques, understanding fabric quality, learning about current fashion trends, and developing an eye for detail.

It's also worth considering formal education in the field. A degree or diploma in fashion design can not only equip you with essential technical skills but also give you a deeper understanding of the fashion industry as a whole.

3.3. Developing a Unique Style

In the world of custom clothing, having a signature style can set you apart. Take some time to consider what kind of clothes you want to specialize in and who your target audience is. Is it bespoke suits for men? Or perhaps custom evening wear for women? Having a niche not only helps you focus and refine your design skills but also makes it easier to market your offering.

3.4. Creating a Business Plan

Once you're confident in your skills and have a clear vision of your target market, it's time to create a business plan. List down all the costs associated with starting your tailoring business – from procurement of raw materials and tools to operational expenses and marketing.

Keep in mind that your business plan is not static, but it should be flexible and adjust as you grow and learn more about your business. In addition, remember to include a financial plan and a contingency plan.

3.5. Setting Up Shop

Next comes setting up your workshop. It could be a physical store or an online platform, or even a combination of both. Consider factors such as location, rental costs, and accessibility to your target customers for a physical store. For an online store, think about website design, ease of navigation, and online marketing strategies.

3.6. Marketing Your Business

No matter how high the quality of your clothes, you need an effective marketing strategy to reach your target customers. Social media platforms, fashion blogs, online and offline advertisements, collaborations with other brands or influencers – these are just some ways to promote your business.

Remember that word-of-mouth referrals are priceless in this industry. So ensure that every customer walks out not just with a beautiful piece of clothing, but also with a wonderful experience.

3.7. Building Customer Relationships

Once your business is established, focus on building strong relationships with your customers. Personalize their experience, be attentive to their needs, and consistently deliver high-quality products. With a loyal customer base, your business won't just survive, it will flourish.

3.8. Continuous Learning and Improvement

The fashion industry is dynamic and trends keep changing. Your ability to adapt to changes and learn constantly will be key to your success. Attend fashion shows, participate in fashion design contests, read fashion magazines, and stay updated with latest trends and technologies.

Transforming your tailoring hobby into a business is not a simple task. It requires hard work, dedication, patience, and passion. But with the right mix of creative talent, business savvy, and a focus on customer satisfaction, your tailoring business can fashion not just clothes, but a legacy of success.

Chapter 4. The Art of Customization: Understanding Bespoke Clothing

Custom tailoring, at its core, underlines the deep connection between a client's personal style and their wardrobe. It starts with listening attentively to your client's desires, visualizing the final design in their specificity, meticulously crafting the piece, and finally delivering a creation that is both unique and a faithful representation of the individual's personality.

4.1. Understanding Bespoke

Bespoke is a term that dates back to the 17th century when people would "speak for," or order, a piece of cloth. Fast forward to modern times, 'bespoke' encapsulates an entire process where clothing items are tailor-made to fit an individual's exact measurements and style preferences, offering a level of customization far beyond an off-the-rack or made-to-measure pieces. Unlike off-the-rack items which provide a standard fit, the bespoke process allows a client to customize from fabric choice, colour, and cut, to individualised detailing and finishings, ensuring a unique piece that fits their body and personality perfectly.

4.2. Personalization in Bespoke Tailoring

One of the critical aspects of bespoke tailoring is personalization. The essence of personalization in bespoke tailoring lies in understanding the client's body - their specific physique and posture, the shape of their body, and the distinct features they wish to highlight or conceal. The choice of fabric, its texture, and color - all these aspects add more depth and character to the clothing.

Every stitch, every thread counts. Each piece speaks volumes about the craftsmanship involved - the care taken in designing, the attention to detail in stitching, maintaining the fineness of seams, scrutinizing the symmetry, and the hand-finishing touch before finally presenting the masterwork to the client. Each bespoke piece is a testament of an artisan's skill and client's unique taste.

4.3. The Creation Process

Bespoke tailoring processes are usually divided into several stages, though this can vary slightly based on the traditions and protocols of different tailoring houses.

1. Consultation: The process begins with a comprehensive discussion about what the client envisions. The bespoke tailor closely listens to the client's expectations, wants, and needs. This is followed by guiding the client in choosing the perfect fabric and style that suits their body, lifestyle, and personality.

2. Measurements: Complete measurements are taken to ensure that the fit is perfect and the clothes match the client's body contours. Measurements usually include specific parts of the body, depending on the clothing item, for instance, around 30 to 50 for a suit.

3. Pattern Creation: After obtaining measurements, a personal pattern is created for the client. This pattern is retained for any future clothing items the client may order.

4. Fittings: Several fittings ensure a precise, comfortable, and aesthetically pleasing fit. The half-made clothes are tested on the client, and alterations are made as necessary.

5. Final Garment: After the last adjustments, the final garment is crafted with thorough attention to every detail. All the findings from the fitting stages are consolidated and the final garment is created.

4.4. Different Styles of Bespoke Tailoring

Bespoke tailoring isn't just about creating well-fitting clothes, it's about crafting clothes that reflect an individual's personality. Styling in bespoke tailoring is greatly influenced by various geopolitical regions, each bringing its distinct flavors and cultural nuances.

1. English Style: Known for its structured fit, the English-style suit boasts a defined shoulder, tapered waist, and a double vent in the back, offering a flattering silhouette.

2. Italian Style: The Italian or Neapolitan style is relaxed and has minimal to no padding, lending a softer and more informal appearance. It includes a rounded shoulder treatment known as "spalla camicia."

3. American Style: American or Ivy League style is a more casual approach to tailoring, typically with a single vent, a straight silhouette, and softer shoulders.

Understanding these styles help in creating a nuanced, personalized piece for each client. It's about shaping an experience, building a style, and not merely customizing a garment.

4.5. The Role of a Bespoke Tailor

A bespoke tailor is more than just a craftsman. The profession demands being a keen listener, a patient observer, and a meticulous creator, all while delivering world-class service. Tailors should be well-versed in different fabrication processes, materials, and, most importantly, the latest fashion trends and classic styles. They serve not only as a tailor but as a style guide and consultant.

This profession demands an eye for detail, exceptional skills in designing and fitting, understanding fabric quality and behavior, knowledge about garment construction, and mastery in pattern-making. To be an efficient tailor, one must be creative and analytical, as tailoring is the art of balancing aesthetics and function.

In the world of bespoke tailoring, the role of the tailor becomes more intimate, bridging the distance between a dream and reality — from an idea in a client's mind to the tangible form of an outfit that impeccably aligns with their personal style and body.

Understanding bespoke clothing is the first significant step in your journey to setting up a successful tailoring business. It's comprehending not just the process of tailoring, but imparting life to threads and fabrics and crafting a narrative that aligns with the client's identity. It's about touching lives, one stitch at a time.

Chapter 5. Learning the Ropes: Essential Tailoring Skills and Techniques

Learning the craft of tailored clothing requires more than just a knack for fashion. It demands an intricate understanding of materials, a mastery of sewing tools, and a discerning eye for detail. The road to tailoring success is paved by the foundational skills and techniques we'll delve into below.

5.1. Understanding Textiles

Before embarking on your tailoring journey, it's vital to familiarize yourself with the heart of any garment – the fabric. Fabric isn't just a medium; it's an element that can make or break your design. Understanding the characteristics of different types of fabrics and how they behave can significantly impact the final outcome of your tailored garment.

1. **Cotton**: Durable, comfortable, and versatile, it's commonly used in shirts, trousers, and casual wear. Its malleability makes it easy to tailor.

2. **Wool**: A breathable fabric perfect for suits. Its elasticity makes it resistant to wrinkles.

3. **Silk**: Luxurious and delicate, reserved for high-end, classy garments. Handling silk requires extra carefulness when tailoring.

4. **Linen**: Light and crisp, perfect for summer wear. It's prone to wrinkles, requiring a deft hand.

5. **Polyester**: A man-made fabric, popular for its durability and easy maintenance. However, its resistance to wrinkles makes tailoring

a bit challenging.

5.2. Tools of the Trade

Crafting a tailor-made garment calls for a set of specialized tools that assist in achieving precise results.

1. **Shears**: Tailors' scissors for cutting fabric, with one pointed and one blunt end.

2. **Seam Ripper**: A tool for removing stitches without imposing damage on the fabric.

3. **Tape Measure**: A flexible ruler to take accurate body and fabric measurements.

4. **Chalk or Marking Pens**: For marking cutting lines or highlighting alterations on the fabric.

5. **Stitching Machine**: For efficient and precise stitching. Models vary, ranging from traditional machines to advanced computerized models.

6. **Iron and Ironing Board**: For pressing clothes during and after crafting to insert creases, flatten seams, and give a finished look.

5.3. Pattern Making and Alteration

One of the most important skills for a tailor to master is pattern making and alteration. At the core, it involves designing, drawing, and cutting a pattern on paper, which is then used as a blueprint for cutting the fabric. Pattern adjustment or alteration is a process of changing pattern pieces to better fit a body's contours, a crucial element in creating bespoke clothing.

1. **Taking Accurate Measurements**: This is the first step in pattern making. Pay close attention to various measurements like chest, waist, hip, and length dimensions, depending on the garment.

2. **Creating Basic Blocks**: Also known as 'slopers', these are representations of the individual body parts, divided region-wise: torso, sleeve, etc.

3. **Drafting the Pattern**: Using the basic blocks, a full pattern is created on paper. This includes adding seam allowances and details like darts, pleats, and fastening placements.

4. **Pattern Grading**: This is a technique to create different sizes of the same pattern, essential when creating a range of sizes for a specific design.

5.4. Sewing Techniques

The essence of tailoring lies in stitching - combining fabric pieces harmoniously using a variety of techniques.

1. **Straight Stitch/Running Stitch**: The most basic and commonly used stitch. It's a simple, straightforward stitch used for most seams.

2. **Back stitch**: This is an extremely sturdy stitch used when strength and stability are required, such as in crotch and armhole seams.

3. **Zigzag Stitch**: Often used to prevent the fabric edges from fraying, or to stitch around buttonholes.

4. **Overlock/Serger Stitch**: A stitch that both seams and finished the edges of the fabric. Usually created with a serger.

5.5. Finishing Touches

Just as crucial as the fabrication and construction of a garment are the finishing touches applied after the main assembly work has been completed.

1. **Pressing**: Ironing the garment to set the stitches, shape the fabric,

and give a finished look. It's often done at multiple stages during tailoring.

2. **Buttonholes and Buttons**: Creating precise buttonholes and attaching the buttons is extremely important for a good finish, and requires practice.

3. **Linings and Interlinings**: These are layers of fabric added inside the garment to enhance its shape and structure. They should be carefully chosen and applied.

Each step in the tailoring process, each skill learned, is an essential bead in the string of your tailoring journey. Learning and mastering these skills and techniques is the first step towards creating that perfectly fitted garment. As you advance, remember - fashion trends might change, but the need for personalized, well-fitted clothing will always remain. Tailoring isn't just a craft; it's an art form that speaks of individuality, precision, and perfection.

Chapter 6. Building Your Brand: Strategies for a Successful Tailoring Business

In the whirlwind of commerce, brand building can serve as the lighthouse in the stormy sea, guiding your tailoring enterprise towards the shore of success. Establishing a compelling brand poised for growth doesn't happen overnight but with patience, diligence, and just the right strategies, your business can carve out a unique niche in the tailoring industry.

6.1. Understanding Your Core Values

Your brand isn't just about your logo, tag line or the colors you incorporate. It goes beyond the tangible and delves into the realm of philosophy. Your brand is a reflection of your company's core values. It's important to understand and articulate the principles and beliefs that underpin your tailoring business.

It's not unusual to find these values rooted in excellence, innovation, customer service, and integrity. Once identified, these shouldn't change as they serve as the moral compass for your business. Your actions, decisions, and business strategies should all align with your defined values. A mismatch between your deeds and professed values could dilute your brand's worth.

6.2. Crafting Your Brand Identity

Tangible elements representing your brand, such as the logo, colors, and typefaces, should be created with meticulous care. Your logo, for instance, ideally should be a visual representation of your company's essentials. Consider the major global brands: their logos effectively capture their ethos in a simple yet potent image.

Color too plays a vital role. According to color psychology, different colors evoke different emotions. Tap into this knowledge to create a color palette that suits your brand's values.

6.3. Defining Your Unique Selling Proposition

With numerous tailors competing for market share, it is crucial to differentiate your business. A unique selling proposition (USP) can build a strong competitive edge. What sets your tailoring business apart? It could be your unrivalled handcrafted quality, quick turnaround times, environmentally friendly materials, or your furtherance of local and traditional tailoring techniques. Whatever it might be, it needs to be unique, believable, and compelling.

6.4. Building and Maintaining Relationships

Relationship-building forms the groundwork for successful branding. Satisfied customers become brand ambassadors, amplifying your reach more effectively and authentically than conventional advertising channels. Provide high-quality products, empathize with customer needs, and deliver excellent after-sales service to form strong bonds.

6.5. Consistent Communication

Once you have defined your brand, you need to express it consistently. All your communication, from website content to social media posts and emails should echo your brand's voice. Consistency not only fosters trust but also reinforces your brand's positioning in the minds of your customers.

6.6. Leveraging Social Media

Exploiting the power of social media for brand building is a strategy that cannot be ignored in the digital age. Use platforms like Instagram or Pinterest, that are visually heavy, to showcase your creations. Facebook and LinkedIn are perfect for testimonials and networking, whereas Twitter can be used for more instantaneous interactions. Remember, each platform requires a slightly modified communication method. Tailor your posts to suit the specific platform's style.

6.7. Respond to Feedback

Customer reviews and feedback offer valuable insights into your operation. Positive feedbacks solidify your brand's credibility, while negative ones provide opportunities for improvement. Make it a practice to respond promptly, and constructively, to all reviews. This builds trust and exemplifies a customer-focused business.

Creating a strong brand in the tailoring industry requires a detailed understanding of your business' ethos, a clear differentiation strategy, and a relentless focus on relationship building. Consistent communication across all marketing channels, the effective use of social media, and a comprehensive feedback response mechanism are additional tools that can propel your brand towards greater heights. Your brand is not merely an identifier but an entire experience—a promise you make to your customers. Make it count.

Chapter 7. Winning the Fabric Race: Sourcing Materials and Supplies

Launch your tailoring venture on the right foot by procuring high-quality materials. Whether it's fabrics, threads, or other essential supplies, you must leave no stone unturned in your pursuit of excellence. Let's delve into the depths of sourcing materials and emphasize the importance of their quality in achieving success in the tailoring industry.

7.1. Know Your Fabrics

Understanding the nuances, differences, and unique traits between various fabrics is crucial. Here are some types you might encounter on your journey.

1. Cotton: Known for its durability and comfort, cotton is versatile and used in various clothing items. It's suitable for different seasons, from hot summer to chilly winters.

2. Silk: Luxurious and elegant, silk is a high-end fabric typically used in finer garments. It's perfect for special occasions or luxurious lines.

3. Wool: Wool is warm, often used in winter garments. It happens to be quite versatile, being used in everything from thick, warm coats to finer, dressier items.

4. Linen: A top choice for summer wear, linen is lightweight and breathable.

5. Synthetic materials: These range from polyester to nylon to spandex. These materials might be more budget-friendly, but they can sometimes lack the comfort and breathability of natural

fibers.

To ensure you're catering to all your potential customers' needs, aim to have a range of these materials available when starting your tailoring business.

7.2. Finding Suppliers

Where you source your fabrics from will directly impact the quality of your final product. Spend time researching suppliers, asking for samples, and scrutinizing every detail. A few renowned fabric marketplaces are the Garment District in New York City, the textile bazaars of Istanbul, the Silk Markets in China, and various other online suppliers and wholesalers.

For threads, buttons, zippers, and other notions, consider creating a network of versatile suppliers. It is advisable to have a primary supplier and a backup option to ensure uninterrupted business operation. Maintain open lines of communication with all your suppliers to facilitate prompt responses to changes in trends or demands.

7.3. Prioritizing Sustainable Sourcing

As today's customers become more conscious of how their decisions impact the environment, sustainable sourcing has become crucial. Organic, ethically-produced fabrics might cost more on the front end, but they often pay dividends in customer loyalty.

Likewise, taking steps to reduce waste can be an effective marketing tool. Implementing a system for reusing fabric scraps or finding vendors who use sustainable shipping methods can demonstrate your commitment to an eco-friendly business.

7.4. Financial Implications

Keeping a close eye on your costs without compromising quality is the key to successful sourcing. Striking a balance will depend on several factors, including the sizes of your orders, your location, and your business model. Consider leveraging economies of scale and negotiating with suppliers for better deals.

7.5. Quality Assurance

Ultimately, the quality of your materials will play a significant role in your tailoring business's overall success. Along with sourcing quality fabrics and supplies, it's critical to develop a stringent quality assurance process to uphold your standards.

7.6. In Conclusion

Winning the fabric race is about much more than just securing supplies for your tailoring business; it's about understanding different fabrics, building relationships with suppliers, exercising financial wisdom, and maintaining a relentless focus on quality. By putting these elements into play, you'll be well on your way to creating a flourishing tailoring business.

Chapter 8. Setting Up Shop: Physical versus Online Stores

Location is one significant aspect when it comes to setting up a tailoring business. Where you set your shop can determine the flow of customers and the growth of your business. In our modern era, businesses generally fall under one of two categories -physical store or an online platform. It's important to understand the merits and challenges of both in establishing a successful tailoring outfit.

8.1. Starting with Physical Store

A physical store refers to an actual, tangible place where businesses offer services or sell products. This traditional model, while seemingly outmoded in some ways, still presents significant advantages for a custom-tailoring outfit.

One of the main benefits of a physical store is that it allows for face-to-face interaction with the clientele. Communication is much more intimate, and it is easier to gauge client needs and preferences. Being able to see and touch the garments allows customers to better appreciate the quality of the work.

Moreover, for a business such as tailoring where measurements need to be accurate, having on-site service can be invaluable. Immediate fitting and adjustments can lead to greater customer satisfaction and increase the likelihood of repeat business.

Physical stores also play an essential role in building a brand and reputation. Having a well-located and beautifully designed shop can help promote your tailoring business. It serves as a physical representation of the kind of service and quality a customer can expect.

On the other hand, there are costs to consider. These include rent, utilities, renovation, and maintenance. Location is critical and can significantly impact the cost. High-traffic locations naturally attract more customers but also carry higher rental costs. Additionally, managing a physical store requires a considerable amount of administration work, which might necessitate hiring additional staff.

8.2. Transitioning to Online Store

A shift is happening in our modern world. Many businesses are now moving online, and many new businesses start within the virtual space, and the tailoring industry is no exception.

An online store allows businesses to reach a wider range of customers. Geographic location is no longer a hindrance. As long as there's internet connection, potential customers can access your shop from anywhere in the world. This increased reach can significantly impact the growth and success of your business.

As for costs, running an online business is usually less expensive than maintaining a physical store. There are no rents to pay, no expensive utility bills, and less staff required. But bear in mind, there are other costs associated with an online store such as website design, maintenance, and marketing.

Trade-off, however, in transition to an online store, is risk of reduced customer interaction and potential difficulty in communication. Additionally, complicated shipping logistics and the inability of customers to touch and feel the fabrics may also present challenges.

8.3. Developing a Hybrid Model

For some, the answer to the online versus physical store conundrum isn't an either-or option. Instead, it's about developing a hybrid model – taking advantage of the best aspects of both worlds.

A hybrid model can involve running a physical store where customers can come for measurements, consultation, and fittings, while also maintaining an online platform for showcasing your portfolio, taking additional orders, servicing overseas clients, and for providing comprehensive customer service.

In a competitive landscape, integrating the traditional and digital approach can potentially be the key to success for your tailoring outfit. It provides the capacity to create a more personalized, immersive shopping experience both online and offline.

However, developing a hybrid model can be complex and resource-intensive. It necessitates robust logistical planning and skilled management.

While there's no one-size-fits-all answer on the best platform to use for your tailoring business, assessing the unique needs of your customer base, the resources you have at your disposal, and the specific goals of your business will guide your decision.

Whether you decide to create a physical store, operate online, or utilize a hybrid model, remember that each platform requires strategic planning to fully realize its potential. Be adaptive, be resilient, and most importantly, be willing to meet the evolving needs of your customers. That's the stitch that holds the fabric of a successful tailoring business.

Indeed, setting up shop for a tailoring business is a journey. The route you choose – whether it be a physical storefront, an online platform, or a combination of both, should be led by careful consideration of your business model, market research, and your clientele's needs. It's a pivotal decision that sets the direction of your entrepreneurial journey in the tailoring industry and could be the difference between prosperity and obscurity.

Remember, every decision about where and how you set up shop determines the seam of your success. So, choose wisely and concretely. After all, it's your craftsmanship on display.

Chapter 9. Keeping the Books: Managing Finance and Operations

Operating a tailoring business successfully isn't solely about mastering your craft but also requires acumen in managing financial and operational aspects of the business. This chapter delves into how to efficiently manage both finance and operations of your tailoring enterprise to ensure you stay on top of your game.

9.1. Financial Planning and Management

The cornerstone of any successful business is its financial health. Getting a solid grasp over your finances as an entrepreneur means knowing how to budget, track expenses, and generate revenues reliably.

A significant consideration in this scenario is to develop a detailed business plan. This plan serves as a blueprint that specifies how you aim to utilize available resources, outlines the costs associated with running your business, and plots your revenue targets.

To keep track of your financial situation, maintaining a regular cash flow statement is essential. This statement encompasses the inflow and outflow of cash, helping identify whether you're making a profit or a loss. In addition, it provides information about upcoming costs and payments, contributing to efficient financial planning.

Moreover, calculating your break-even point is a useful exercise that allows you to identify when your business is expected to start making a profit. It involves taking into account your fixed costs, variable costs, and the selling price of your service.

Understanding and controlling your costs is critical in business. In tailoring, the major types of costs you will encounter include material costs, labor costs, overhead costs (e.g., electricity, rent), and marketing costs. Keep a keen eye on these costs, and incorporate efficient cost-saving measures wherever possible.

9.2. Operations Management

Pay attention not only to your financials but also to your operational efficiency. How smoothly your business runs daily can significantly influence your profitability.

Key routine operations include the management of customer orders, workflow efficiency, quality controls, and customer service. Streamlining these operations can heighten productivity and customer satisfaction, thereby improving your business performance.

Developing an efficient workflow process is paramount. Break down each task in your business and get to know each step's timing. This way, you understand how long it takes for an order to be processed and completed, and you can manage customer expectations more effectively.

Quality control measures are essential in maintaining your brand's reputation. Regularly checking your work for consistency and quality not only ensures customer satisfaction but also minimizes costly redoing or adjustments.

Customer service also plays a significant role in your operation's success. Establish good communication with your clients to manage their expectations and handle queries or complaints.

Consider investing in technology to automate and streamline certain processes like stock control, order management, bookkeeping, and customer relationship management. This can help reduce manual errors and free up your time to focus on aspects of your business that require your unique skills as a tailor.

9.3. Taxation and Legal Consideration

Understanding the legalities and tax obligations associated with running a small business is critical. Consult with professionals to ensure you're adhering to the legal standards of your location. Areas to keep in view are business registration, permits and licenses, employment laws, and the like.

Also, familiarize yourself with your tax obligations. These may vary depending on circumstances like your business structure, location, and the number of employees. It is vital to understand your liability for sales tax, income tax, and employee taxes.

In conclusion, while the art of tailoring is about creating pieces that fit perfectly, successfully running a tailoring business is about fitting different pieces of management, finance, and operations into a unified whole. It's about watching the numbers while also nurturing craftsmanship, balancing creativity with practicality.

Chapter 10. Marketing Your Craftsmanship: Advertising in the Bespoke Clothing Industry

In this competitive world of fashion, marketing your custom tailoring business stands as a critical task. Not only does it help in enhancing your brand identity, but it also gains the attention of your prospective audience, leading to increased income and growth prospects.

10.1. Understanding Your Target Audience:

Understanding your target audience is the first step to make effective marketing strategies. It is crucial to have a clear picture of who you would be catering to. Are they young professionals who want unique office wear? Are they brides-to-be looking for the perfect wedding dress? Are they fashion-forward individuals willing to spend a premium on personal expression?

Once you ascertain your target customers' demographics, preferences, behaviors, and consumer habits, you can design a marketing strategy geared towards their specific needs and preferences.

10.2. Creating a Unique Brand Identity:

A significant aspect of marketing your craftsmanship revolves around creating a unique brand identity that makes you stand apart.

Your brand identity is the voice that speaks to your audience on your behalf. When crafting your brand identity, consider these fundamental elements:

1. Your brand purpose - why does your brand exist?

2. Your brand promise - what do you pledge to deliver to your clients?

3. Your brand personality - if your brand were a person, who would they be?

Remember, consistency is the key when it comes to maintaining a brand identity. From your logo to your communication style, to the materials you use, everything should resonate with your core brand values.

10.3. Building a Website and Portfolio:

Living in the digital age, owning a functional and visually appealing website is an absolute necessity for your tailoring business. Your website should include an about us section, outlining your journey and values, a portfolio to showcase your skill and creativity, and contact details for potential clients to reach out to you.

Your portfolio should be more than just a collection of photos. It should tell a story about your work, showcasing your ability to understand client needs and translate it into impeccable clothing pieces.

10.4. Leveraging Social Media:

Social media can serve as a powerful tool for marketing your bespoke tailoring business. Platforms such as Facebook, Instagram, and Pinterest, are not just channels for showcasing your work, but they also help you interact with your audience on a more personal level.

Instagram, especially with its visually-driven nature, is an ideal platform for tailors. Use Instagram stories, reels, and IGTV to show your design process, client fittings, before-and-afters, and more. These actions not only promote your work, but also provide a glimpse of the person behind the business, creating a connection with your audience.

10.5. Networking and Partnerships:

Networking is vital for your business growth. It gives you the opportunity to meet potential clients, business partners, and mentors. Attend fashion events, business seminars, and trade shows to meet like-minded people, share your business cards, and expand your network.

Additionally, establishing partnerships with businesses that complement yours can also be a strategic move. For example, partnering with wedding planners or professional stylists can help bring in a steady flow of customers.

10.6. Involvement with Fashion Shows and Events:

Getting involved with fashion shows and events can help put your brand in the spotlight. It offers an excellent platform to showcase your work to a larger audience. Remember to follow up such events with press releases, professional photos, and thorough coverage on your social media platforms to keep the momentum going.

10.7. Customer Service and Referral Programs:

Lastly, never underestimate the power of word-of-mouth marketing. Happy customers spread the word, playing a crucial part in advertising your business. Providing excellent customer service, meeting deadlines, and creating superior clothes are fundamental.

Moreover, you could introduce referral programs where your clients receive discounts or benefits when they successfully refer someone. This way, you not only retain your existing clientele but also attract new ones.

Remember, marketing your craftsmanship is an ongoing process, requiring patience and consistency. It's not just about advertising, but building relationships, conveying your brand message, and ensuring customer satisfaction. With the right strategies, your bespoke tailoring business can reach greater heights and achieve remarkable success.

Chapter 11. Sustaining Success: Growth and Expansion of Your Tailoring Business

Every craft has its secrets and strategies, so does tailoring. Once you've established a foundation for your tailoring business, the next key step is sustainable growth and expansion. To excel, understanding the dynamics of the industry, utilizing the right promotional methods, tackling challenges, and implementing effective expansion plans is obligatory.

11.1. Crafting a Growth Strategy

The first tactical advancement towards success is establishing a robust growth strategy. As a part of this plan, keep a close eye on your financials. A clear understanding of the inflow and outflow of your cash helps to gauge and enhance the financial longevity of your enterprise. It is advisable to use software-based financial planning tools to assess both your short-term results and long-term viability.

Under the banner of growth, seeking new partnerships is crucial too. Collaborating with local boutiques, designers, and other businesses can open up a multitude of opportunities. Joining industry associations can also provide the added benefit of accessing an entire network of potential joint venture partners.

11.2. Balancing Quality and Quantity

It's common to overlook the importance of quality when striving for growth, but this approach can be detrimental. Balancing quality and quantity is a fundamental concern here. Staying consistent in delivering high-quality, personalized garments requires a focused endeavor.

Ultimately, it's your craftsmanship that attracts customers, and upholding this standard should be a primary objective. Wielding this balance also involves managing your labor force effectively. Cater to your staffing needs wisely, considering the balance between experienced hands and apprentices for cost efficiency and quality assurance.

11.3. Embracing Technological Advances

Another important facet of the growth phase is embracing technological progress. Use of technology in your tailoring business can help you stay competitive. Use software for everything - from managing inventory to scheduling orders and payments.

Also, leveraging online presence is essential. Running social media campaigns and maintaining an engaging, accessible online presence can aid in extending your outreach beyond geographical boundaries.

11.4. Facing Challenges Head-On

Every growth phase comes with its share of challenges, facing them head-on is critical for business sustenance. This could range from managing tight deadlines and handling increased workloads to ensuring client satisfaction and maintaining high quality standards.

Being prepared for unforeseen circumstances and reacting promptly to issues will equip you to manage these challenges adeptly. A proactive approach can go a long way in dealing with setbacks. Keep an eye on the market dynamics, consumer behavior, and competitors' moves.

11.5. Expansion Plans: Branching Out vs. Diversification

When it comes to expansion, there are two primary paths you can take - opening new branches or diversifying your services.

Starting additional outlets in new locations can help reach more customers directly. Nevertheless, this move requires substantial investment and careful market research to ensure the branch's viability.

Diversification, meanwhile, entails expanding your services or product line. From introducing bespoke accessories or offering wardrobe consultation to premium fabric sourcing, the possibilities here are unlimited. However, before diversification, conducting market research and customer surveys to understand demand is paramount.

11.6. Conclusion: Achieving Long-Term Success

Sustaining success in a tailoring business calls for an intricate blend of maintaining traditional craftsmanship and adopting modern business designs. Effectively balancing growth while upholding quality, embracing technology, and navigating challenges lays the road to expansion and sustained success.

The sartorial journey undoubtedly takes effort and endurance but remember, "The only place where success comes before work is in the dictionary." So, stitch your dreams carefully, measure your steps wisely, and snip away all doubts. It's time to button up and be ready for the next step of your tailoring business venture.

www.ingramcontent.com/pod-product-compliance
Lightning Source LLC
Chambersburg PA
CBHW060857260726
48661CB00008B/3310